Pause And Breathe

10 Mindfulness Scripts for Anyone in Any Moment

Lisa Hamer Jenkins

Table of Contents

DEDICATION

To my children, JJ and Ellie.

My heart overflows with love and pride for you.

ACKNOWLEDGMENTS

I am very blessed to have a strong circle of support.

Thank you to my family –

My husband Jamison, for a 30-year adventure filled with lots of love and countless unexpected twists and turns.

My children, JJ and Ellie, for teaching me way more than I've taught you.

My parents, Dale and Arden Hamer, and my sister Megan Tomley for your endless love and encouragement.

Thank you to Team Muscle – Coach Dana, Justin, Allie, Nicole, and Rae for always pushing me to go a little further and reminding me to never give up on my goals.

Thank you to God, who guides me on every step of life's journey.

ABOUT THE AUTHOR

Mindfulness has been a part of Lisa Hamer Jenkins' life in many capacities. Personally, Lisa has practiced mindfulness to reduce stress, battle food cravings and promote sleep. She has shared mindfulness with her family to manage pain and battle anxiety. Throughout her 25-year career as a social worker Lisa has used mindfulness in various settings with her clients. Having a mindfulness script on hand helps her to be ready at any moment in any situation to offer those she is helping the opportunity to pause and breathe.

Life moves amazingly fast.

It is easy to get wrapped up in the moment and not even notice that life's moving. Or we allow things like worry, anxiety, pain, cravings, or emotions to put the brakes on, and we're frozen in time.

If we give ourselves the opportunity to breathe, we can allow life to pause. We can then purposefully make the choice to feel what we want, respond how we want, or simply enjoy the moment.

We can also give our clients, students, patients, or family members this same opportunity. The opportunity to pause... breathe... and purposefully make a choice on their next move or their next thought.

Pausing to breathe by doing a simple mindfulness exercise brings our attention to the present moment. It helps us to observe, identify and explore our thoughts and emotions.

Practicing mindfulness can impact our physical, mental, and emotional health in many ways. The regular practice of mindfulness will have the greatest impact, but even doing a one-time exercise can bring calm to that moment. In the moment, mindfulness can impact health in ways such as decreasing feelings of stress, promoting calm, increasing focus, reducing pain, lowering heart rate, encouraging sleep, and helping to fight cravings.

Life feels too big. I'm anxious. I'm too scared to make a move.

Let's pause and breathe to bring calm and focus.

I'm so nervous about this math test. I can't think straight.

Let's pause and breathe before we start this test.

What do I do when I desperately want to smoke a cigarette or eat another cookie?

Let's pause and breathe to fight off that craving before you pick up a cigarette or cookie.

My pain is getting worse. I don't think I can take it.

Let's pause and breathe to see if we can reduce that pain.

This booklet contains ten simple mindfulness scripts that can be used in a multitude of situations regardless of where you are – a classroom, an office, a hospital room, or a home. You do not need any special equipment or supplies. Just your voice sharing the words bringing the gift of a moment to the one you are helping.

Lisa Hamer Jenkins

Pause And Breath

INSTRUCTIONS

Have the person you are working with sit or lay in a comfortable position. If possible, remove all distractions, such as turning off the TV, silencing your cell phones, or closing the door. In a calm, gentle voice, slowly read the script.

Where it says <PAUSE>, I often slowly count to five or ten silently to myself to help me hold the pause and not rush through it.

Depending on the setting that you are in when you are done, you can:

- Transition right into the activity you have planned, such as taking a test, beginning a procedure, or starting a meeting
- Allow the person to remain where they are and rest. This is especially good if the person is experiencing pain or is having trouble sleeping
- Ask the person reflective questions such as:
- How are you feeling?

- Tell me how you feel now versus before the mindfulness practice

- Was this helpful for you? Tell me about it

- What did you see as I was reading? Smell? Hear?

- What thoughts or memories came to mind during the practice?

When the person is ready to stand up, have them get up slowly to give their mind and body the chance to orient back to the present moment.

GUIDED BREATHING

I invite you to join me for a guided breathing mindfulness practice.

Take a deep breath in through your nose.

Slowly exhale through your mouth.

Deep breath in.

Exhale.

Let's prepare our bodies for this practice.

Allow your body to sink into a comfortable position. If you choose, close your eyes. Rest your hands gently in your lap or at your side. Continue to take deep breaths as you give your entire body permission to relax.

Your forehead.

Your jaw.

Your neck.

Your shoulders.

Your spine.

Your stomach.

Your thighs.

Your ankles.

Relax from your head to your toes.

Breathe now at your own pace.

Envision the air entering through your nose or mouth, flowing through your entire body, and then leaving your body.

Concentrate on each breath as you breathe in and out.

<PAUSE>

We are going to take in several deep breaths counting to five, holding for two, and then exhaling over a count of five. Each one at the height of the inhale. Breathe in through your nose and out through your mouth. Concentrate on each breath.

Allow the air you breathe in to fill your belly, causing it to expand and contract with each breath. Keep your shoulders still and relaxed.

If a thought should enter your mind, don't dwell on it. Simply acknowledge it and let it pass. Return your focus to the flow of your breath. In and out.

<PAUSE>

Let's begin.

Take in a slow deep breath as I count

1... 2... 3... 4... 5...

Hold your breath for 1… 2…

Slowly and fully release your breath as I count

1... 2... 3... 4.... 5...

Continue.

Take in a slow deep breath as I count

1... 2... 3... 4... 5...

Hold your breath for 1… 2…

Slowly and fully release your breath as I count

1... 2... 3... 4... 5...

Take in a slow deep breath as I count

1... 2... 3... 4... 5...

Hold your breath for 1…2…

Slowly and fully release your breath as I count

1... 2... 3... 4... 5...

Take in a slow deep breath as I count

1... 2... 3... 4... 5...

Hold your breath for 1… 2…

Slowly and fully release your breath as I count

1... 2... 3... 4... 5...

Take in a slow deep breath as I count

1... 2... 3... 4... 5...

Hold your breath for 1...2...

Slowly and fully release your breath as I count

1... 2... 3... 4... 5...

Take in a slow deep breath as I count

1... 2... 3... 4... 5...

Hold your breath for 1... 2...

Slowly and fully release your breath as I count

1... 2... 3... 4... 5...

Take in a slow deep breath as I count

1... 2... 3... 4... 5...

Hold your breath for 1... 2...

Slowly and fully release your breath as I count

1... 2... 3... 4... 5...

Take in a slow deep breath as I count

1... 2... 3... 4... 5...

Hold your breath for 1... 2...

Slowly and fully release your breath as I count

1... 2... 3... 4... 5...

Take in a slow deep breath as I count

1... 2... 3... 4... 5...

Hold your breath for 1... 2...

Slowly and fully release your breath as I count

1... 2... 3... 4... 5...

One final time.

Take in a slow deep breath as I count

1... 2... 3... 4... 5...

Hold your breath for 1... 2...

Slowly and fully release your breath as I count

1... 2... 3... 4... 5...

Allow your breathing to return to your normal pattern.

Rest in this place for a while longer.

<PAUSE>

It's time to return our focus to the present moment.

Open your eyes.

Wiggle your fingers.

Wiggle your toes.

Face the rest of your day feeling peaceful and energized.

DEEP BREATHING - TEN COUNT

I invite you to join me for a guided breathing mindfulness practice.

Take a deep breath in through your nose.

Slowly exhale through your mouth.

Deep breath in.

Exhale.

Let's prepare our bodies for this practice.

Find a comfortable position in your chair. If you choose, close your eyes.

Starting with your neck, gently and slowly tilt your head from side to side, taking your right ear to your shoulder, feeling a slight stretch. Then your left ear to your shoulder. Back to the right and then to the left. Back to center.

Move your focus to your shoulders. Slowly lift your shoulders up towards your ears, feeling a slight stretch. And back down. Lift up. And down.

Take your hands and make a fist. Straighten your fingers and stretch them out, opening your hand as wide as you can. Make a fist. Open your hand, stretching your fingers. Rest your hands gently in your lap or at your side.

Focusing on your legs and feet, slowly march in place, lifting your left foot. Set in down. Lift your right foot. Set it down. Left. Right.

Find a comfortable position in your chair as we will turn our focus to our breathing.

Breathe now at your own pace.

Envision the air entering through your nose or mouth, flowing through your entire body, and then leaving your body.

Concentrate on each breath, and you breathe in and out.

If a thought should enter your mind, do not dwell on it. Simply acknowledge it and let it pass. Return your focus to the flow of your breath. In and out.

<PAUSE>

Feel your chest and stomach rise and fall with each breath.

Notice the coolness of the air as it enters your body and its warmth as it leaves.

Feel your body relaxing.

<PAUSE>

We're going to take ten deep breaths counting each one at the height of the inhale. Breathe in through your nose and out through your mouth. Concentrate on each breath, counting along with me.

Let's begin.

Take in a deep breath, as deep as you can.

At the height of your breath in count – One

Slowly and fully release your breath.

Take in another deep breath – as deep as you can.

At the height of your breath in count – Two

Slowly and fully release your breath.

Breathe in – Three

Release.

Breathe in – Four

Release.

Breathe in – Five

Release.

Breathe in – Six

Release.

Breathe in – Seven

Release.

Breathe in – Eight

Release.

Breathe in – Nine

Release.

Breathe in – Ten

Release.

Allow your breathing to return to your normal pattern.

How are you feeling?

Is your body relaxed? Is your mind calm?

Rest in this place for a while longer.

<PAUSE>

It's time to return our focus to the present moment.

Open your eyes.

Wiggle your fingers.

Wiggle your toes.

Face the rest of your day feeling peaceful and energized.

BODY SCAN

I invite you to join me for a guided body scan mindfulness practice.

Find a comfortable position – whether it's sitting or lying down. Gently place your hands on your stomach or at your side. Close your eyes or softly focus on an area in front of you.

Take several long deep breaths inhaling through your nose, exhaling through your mouth.

<PAUSE>

Allow your breathing to return to its normal pattern.

Allow the outside world to fade away.

If a thought drifts into your mind, simply acknowledge it, and on your next exhale, blow through pursed lips blowing that thought from your mind. Let it float away and return your focus to your breathing.

On your next breath, begin to focus on the sensation of the air entering through your nose and flowing through your entire body. Imagine little bubbles containing warmth and relaxation floating through that air as it moves through you.

As you exhale, allow your body to soften and relax.

<PAUSE>

Take your focus from your breath and place it on your feet. Notice the sensation of your feet touching the surface below it. Wiggle your toes. How do your feet feel? Do you have any pain or tension, or burning in your feet? Are your feet hot or cold? On your next inhale, imagine those little bubbles floating down to your feet and replacing any discomfort with soothing warmth and a sense of relaxation. Allow your feet to relax.

Move your focus up to your ankles. What sensations do you feel here? On your next inhale, imagine those little bubbles floating down to circle your ankles, replacing any discomfort with soothing warmth and a sense of relaxation. Allow your ankles to relax.

Move your focus up to your knees. How do your knees feel? Do you feel any discomfort or tightness? On your next inhale, imagine those little bubbles floating down to circle your knees, replacing any discomfort with soothing warmth and a sense of relaxation. Allow your knees to relax.

Move your focus to your legs – your calves and your thighs. Feel them resting against the surface you are on. What sensations do you feel in your legs? Do they feel heavy? Tight? Do they feel weak? On your next inhale, imagine those little bubbles floating to your legs, flowing up and down, replacing any discomfort with soothing warmth and a sense of relaxation. Allow your legs to relax.

Move your focus to your lower back and pelvis. What sensations do you feel here? Continue to move your focus up your spine to your middle and upper back. How do your muscles feel? Are they filled with tension? Do you feel pain? On your next inhale, imagine those little bubbles flowing up and down your spine, replacing any discomfort with soothing warmth and a sense of relaxation. Allow your spine to relax.

Move your focus to your stomach and your chest. Notice your stomach rise and fall with each breath. Feel the beating of your heart. What sensations do you feel here? On your next inhale, imagine those little bubbles filling your stomach and chest, replacing any discomfort with soothing warmth and a sense of relaxation. Allow your stomach and chest to relax.

Move your focus to your shoulders. How do your shoulders feel? Are they tight? Do they ache? On your next inhale, imagine those little bubbles dancing around your shoulders, replacing any discomfort with soothing warmth and a sense of relaxation. Allow your shoulders to relax.

Move your focus to your arms. What sensation do you feel in your arms? How do your elbows feel? On your next inhale, imagine those little bubbles flowing up and down your arms wrapping around your elbows, replacing any discomfort with soothing warmth and a sense of relaxation. Allow your arms to relax.

Move your focus to your hands and your wrists. How do they feel? Do they ache? Do they feel stiff? Are they hot or cold? On your next inhale, imagine those little bubbles moving around your wrists before gathering in your hands and flowing up and down each finger, replacing any discomfort with soothing warmth and a sense of relaxation. Allow your hands and wrists to relax.

Move your focus to your neck. What sensations do your feel here? On your next inhale, imagine those little bubbles circulating around your neck, replacing any discomfort with soothing warmth and a sense of relaxation. Allow your neck to relax.

Move your focus to your head. What sensations do you feel here? Notice the point of contact of the back of your head to the chair or pillow. Focus on your jaw. Is it tight? Are you grinding your teeth? Focus on your eyes. Are you squinting or holding any tension in your eyes? On your next inhale, imagine those little bubbles flowing through your head, replacing any discomfort with soothing warmth and a sense of relaxation. Allow your head to relax.

Spread your focus to your entire body. Imagine the little bubbles flowing throughout. Embrace the feeling of comfort and warmth and relaxation.

Stay in this moment for a while. Breathing gently.

<PAUSE>

When you are ready, return your focus to the present moment.

Slowly open your eyes.

Take one final deep breath through your nose. Exhale through your mouth.

Wiggle your fingers.

Wiggle your toes.

Rest here for just a moment before getting up, ready to face the rest of your day with a body that is feeling warm and relaxed.

BODY SCAN II

I invite you to join me for a guided body scan mindfulness practice.

Take a deep breath in through your nose.

Slowly exhale through your mouth.

Deep breath in.

Exhale.

Deep breath in.

Exhale.

Allow your body to sink into a comfortable position. If you choose, close your eyes. Rest your hands gently in your lap or at your side. Continue to take deep breaths as you give your entire body permission to relax.

Relax your forehead.

Deep breath in.

Exhale.

Relax your jaw.

Deep breath in.

Exhale.

Relax your neck.

Deep breath in.

Exhale.

Relax your shoulders.

Deep breath in.

Exhale.

Relax your arms.

Deep breath in.

Exhale.

Relax your hands.

Deep breath in.

Exhale.

Relax your spine.

Deep breath in.

Exhale.

Relax your stomach.

Deep breath in.

Exhale.

Relax your thighs.

Deep breath in.

Exhale.

Relax your calves.

Deep breath in.

Exhale.

Relax your ankles.

Deep breath in.

Exhale.

Relax your toes.

Deep breath in.

Exhale.

Rest here

In this moment

Your body relaxed from head to toe.

Deep breath in.

Exhale.

Deep breath in.

Exhale.

<PAUSE>

When you are ready, return your focus to the present moment.

Open your eyes.

Wiggle your fingers.

Wiggle your toes.

Face the rest of your day relaxed.

I AM LOVED * I GIVE LOVE

I invite you to join me for a Mindfulness Practice that focuses on love – love for ourselves, the love we receive from others, and the love that we share with others.

Take a deep breath through your nose.

Slowly exhale through your mouth.

Deep breath in.

Exhale.

Let's prepare our bodies for this practice.

Allow your body to sink into a comfortable position. If you choose, close your eyes. Rest your hands gently in your lap or at your side. Continue to take deep breaths as you give your entire body permission to relax.

Your forehead.

Your jaw.

Your neck.

Your shoulders.

Your spine.

Your stomach.

Your thighs.

Your ankles.

Relax from your head to your toes.

Breathe now at your own pace.

Envision the air entering through your nose or mouth, flowing through your entire body, and then leaving your body.

Concentrate on each breath as you breathe in and out.

<PAUSE>

Place your hand on your heart, and feel the rhythmic beating.

Take a few breaths just to delight in the thump, thump, thump of your heart, the pure feeling of being alive. Inhale. Exhale.

<PAUSE>

Now imagine that you are surrounded on all sides by all the people who love you and have loved you and whom you love. Picture all your friends and loved ones surrounding you. They are sending you wishes for your happiness, well-being, and health. Bask in the warm wishes and love coming from all sides. You are filled to overflowing.

<PAUSE>

Focus back on your breathing. As you inhale, picture thousands of tiny red hearts dancing in the air that you are breathing in. Take a few steady, even breaths, your lungs expanding as they fill with tiny red hearts. Expand your belly, filling it with red hearts as you inhale. Imagine yourself drawing in all the love from those around you.

On the exhales, feel your chest fall as you let all the breath out, gently blowing red hearts out into the world. Imagine yourself sending out love to all of those around you.

Inhale love from others.

Exhale love to others.

Inhale love from others.

Exhale love to others.

Now place your hands on your knees or in your lap. Continue breathing deeply.

As you inhale, say to yourself, "I am," and as you exhale, say to yourself, "loved". Then as you inhale, say to yourself, "I give," and as you exhale, say to yourself, "love."

Complete a few rounds of this exercise, inhaling "I am" and exhaling "loved". Inhaling "I give", exhaling "love."

I am . . . loved.

I give . . . love.

One more time

I am . . . loved.

I give . . . love.

Pause to cherish this moment of being loved and giving love.

<PAUSE>

Return your focus to your breath.

Take a deep breath in through your nose.

Slowly exhale through your mouth.

Deep breath in.

Exhale.

Deep breath in.

Exhale.

When you are ready, return your focus to the present moment.

Open your eyes.

Wiggle your fingers.

Wiggle your toes.

Face the rest of your day with a heart filled with love.

SELF-COMPASSION

I invite you to join me today for a guided self-compassion mindfulness practice. Before we focus on self-compassion, let's pause and prepare our minds and body for the practice.

Take a deep breath in through your nose.

Slowly exhale through your mouth.

Deep breath in.

Exhale.

Deep breath in.

Exhale.

Allow your body to sink into a comfortable position. If you choose, close your eyes. Rest your hands gently in your lap or at your side. Continue to take deep breaths as you give your entire body permission to relax.

Your forehead.

Your jaw.

Your neck.

Your shoulders.

Your spine.

Your stomach.

Your thighs.

Your ankles.

Relax from your head to your toes.

Focus your attention back to your breathing.

Deep breath in.

Exhale.

Deep breath in.

Exhale.

If it is comfortable for you, place one or both of your hands over your heart. Do you feel the beat of your heart?

Continue with feeling the rhythm of your heartbeat and your even deep breathing as you listen.

Self-compassion is recognizing when we are going through a rough time, such as when we have failed at something, when we are not physically feeling well or when we see something we don't like about ourselves, and treating ourselves with love and respect, and kindness. Self-compassion is not judging or criticizing. Self-compassion is giving ourselves grace.

Sometimes the self-talk we hear in our head is not a very loving or respectful, or kind voice. We can really beat ourselves up with the way we talk to ourselves. Our own words to ourselves can be mean and hurtful.

Today we are going to listen to and repeat several self-affirming statements to help change our negative self-talk into compassionate self-talk. As we take a deep breath in, I am going to say a statement. As we exhale, you repeat that statement. It's up to you if you want to repeat it quietly in your mind or say it out loud. Either way works fine. During the first few statements, you will hear me quietly repeating to demonstrate the process. We will repeat the series of four statements three times.

Let's begin.

You may keep your hands over your heart or return them to your lap or side. Whatever is comfortable for you.

Focus your attention back to your breathing.

Deep breath in.

Exhale.

Deep breath in.

Exhale.

Breathe in

I am strong

Exhale

(I am strong)

Breathe in

I am brave

Exhale

(I am brave)

Breathe in

I am resilient

Exhale

(I am resilient)

Breathe in

I believe in me

Exhale

(I believe in me)

Breathe in

I am strong

Exhale

Breath in

I am brave

Exhale

Breathe in

I am resilient

Exhale

Breathe in

I believe in me

Exhale

Breathe in

I am strong

Exhale

Breath in

I am brave

Exhale

Breathe in

I am resilient

Exhale

Breathe in

I believe in me

Exhale

Continue with your deep, even breathing.

The next time that you find your self-talk tearing you down with negative statements, you can tell yourself to stop it. Close your eyes. Take a few deep breaths. And repeat those four statements.

I am strong.

I am brave.

I am resilient.

I believe in myself.

Treat yourself with love and respect, and kindness.

Have compassion for yourself.

Take a few final deep breaths.

Deep breath in.

Exhale.

Deep breath in.

Exhale

When you are ready, return your focus to the present moment.

Open your eyes.

Wiggle your fingers.

Wiggle your toes.

Face the rest of your day with a heart filled with love, respect, and kindness for you.

GUIDED IMAGERY: THE BEACH

I invite you to join me for a Guided Imagery Mindfulness Practice. Allow your body to relax while your mind escapes to the beach.

Take a deep breath in through your nose.

Slowly exhale through your mouth.

Deep breath in.

Exhale.

Deep breath in.

Exhale.

Allow your body to sink into a comfortable position. If you choose, close your eyes. Rest your hands gently in your lap or at your side. Continue to take deep breaths as you give your entire body permission to relax.

Relax from your head to your toes.

Focus your attention back to your breathing.

Deep breath in.

Exhale.

Deep breath in.

Exhale.

Now picture yourself standing outside on the top step of a rustic wooden staircase. This staircase has allowed you to climb over a small sand dune – a hill of sand covered in tall green blades of beach grass.

It's very early in the morning. The sky is a light grey. The sun is still asleep. You know that the moon remains visible in the sky behind you, but you don't turn to look. You can't tear your eyes away from the anticipated beauty that will soon be before you. You don't want to miss a single second.

You can see and hear the ocean waves crashing against the shore.

There is a cool breeze. You feel it softly blowing against your cheek like a sweet good morning kiss. You are thankful you put on your favorite sweater. The warmth it provides pairs a comforting hug with that sweet kiss. You take a deep breath in, soaking in this moment.

Slowly, you begin to descend the steps. Your right hand slides down the handrail – the wood is smooth, softened by the touch of thousands of hands who have made this early morning journey before you. Were their hearts filled with the amount of happiness that fills yours in this moment?

Reaching the bottom step, you pause and kick your flip-flops into the beach grass. Balancing on your left leg, you point the toes on your right foot and gently dip down, swinging your leg back and forth, allowing your toes to glide gently across the cool soft sand.

After a few seconds, you step fully into the sand and begin walking towards the shore. The cold sand covers your feet and slides in between your toes. It's low tide. You see an uneven line of seashells and stones winding its way down the beach parallel to the shore where the high tide had left them hours before. Among the shells and stones are clumps of green and brown seaweed that have also washed ashore. You watch sand crabs of all sizes silently zipping around before disappearing into the holes they have dug in the sand.

You stop right before the soft sand transitions to sand that is still firm and wet from last night's high tide. There are a few other people who have come to the beach this morning to experience this gift from nature. Everyone is spread out along the shore, some standing, some sitting, but all in silence. Waiting.

Spreading your blanket out, you take a seat and take in a very deep breath. The salty air fills your lungs as you pause again to purposely soak in this moment.

Your timing is perfect.

Just at that moment, a light-yellow line starts to illuminate the horizon. There is a deep contrast between that yellow and the grey that remains of the nighttime sky.

For the first time that morning, you notice the birds. Seagulls – some flying solo, some in colonies – take off and land on the sand around you. Their short staccato squawking is a drum beat against the smooth melody of the crashing waves. Squadrons of pelicans fly out over the water. A straight line follows the leader climbing high into the sky and then floating down to glide close to the water. Every once in a while, one will break from the group, diving straight down and disappearing into the ocean. They've found a fish!

Your eyes return to the horizon. The light-yellow light has pushed the grey higher into the sky. The horizon is now glowing a bright lemon yellow. You don't dare move your gaze from that spot where the sky meets the water far out in the ocean. You take a deep breath in through your nose and slowly exhale.

Then there it is.

The very top curve of a glimmering golden-yellow sphere has appeared.

Slowly it rises.

A vivid shade of orange spreads across the sky as if lifting the golden sun to its glory. The reflection of the sun creates a stripe across the water from the horizon to the shore as if reaching out directly to you. Your heart is filled with joy.

The sun, though still not fully visible, is so bright that you can hardly look directly at it. You turn your attention to the multiple shades of yellow and orange that now paint the sky. The color of the water has changed in the sun's reflection to a deep blue. The white caps of the crashing waves sparkle under the rays of the rising sun.

The beauty before you is incredible. You don't know how you will be able to describe it to anyone, but that's ok. This is your moment. Everything else has disappeared.

It is just you and the rising sun.

You and a brand-new day.

You and an endless amount of hope and inspiration.

You watch in awe as the sun climbs completely above the horizon, spreading its full light across the sky and the ocean. You can feel the warmth of the rays brushing your cheeks. Another sweet good morning kiss.

Taking in a deep breath, you know it is time to go.

You stare out over the horizon one last time attempting to memorize every color and, more importantly, hoping to tuck all the emotions – happiness, joy, hope – deep into your heart so that you can reflect on this moment whenever you need to escape.

You slowly rise to your feet, pulling your blanket up with you, your gaze never leaving the water. You shake off the sand, fold the blanket and tuck it under your arm.

Before you can change your mind, you turn and walk back to the steps.

The sand feels warmer under your feet.

You find your flip-flops on the beach grass and climb the steps.

You want to turn and look back one more time, but you don't.

Instead, you head down the steps on the other side of the dune.

Life awaits.

Return your focus to your breath.

Take a deep breath in through your nose.

Slowly exhale through your mouth.

Deep breath in.

Exhale.

Deep breath in.

Exhale. Take a deep breath in.

When you are ready, return your focus to the present moment.

Open your eyes.

Wiggle your fingers.

Wiggle your toes.

Face the rest of your day with a heart filled with happiness, joy, and hope.

GUIDED IMAGERY: A CITY PARK

I invite you to join me for a Guided Imagery Mindfulness Practice. Allow your body to relax while your mind escapes to a city park.

Take a deep breath in through your nose.

Slowly exhale through your mouth.

Deep breath in.

Exhale.

Deep breath in.

Exhale.

Allow your body to sink into a comfortable position. If you choose, close your eyes. Rest your hands gently in your lap or at your side. Continue to take deep breaths as you give your entire body permission to relax.

Your forehead.

Your jaw.

Your neck.

Your shoulders.

Your spine.

Your stomach.

Your thighs.

Your ankles.

Relax from your head to your toes.

Focus your attention back to your breathing.

Deep breath in.

Exhale.

Deep breath in.

Exhale.

Now picture yourself standing on a busy street corner on the edge of downtown. You are surrounded by tall buildings. Cars and buses fly by you on the street. You hear horns beeping and people talking. A low thumping beat comes from one of the cars as it slowly makes a turn in front of you. You smell a mixture of fumes and dust. The speed of the passing vehicles combined with the wind tunnel created by the buildings causes empty cups, napkins, and other garbage to blow along the sidewalk. Standing with a group of people in the shadows of the buildings, you are all waiting for the stop light to turn green, giving your permission to safely cross the street. Waiting. Watching. Silently willing that light to turn green.

As soon as that light turns, you take off, pushing your way to the front of the crowd and crossing to the other side of the street. You briskly walk down the sidewalk leaving everyone behind. Your destination is just a block away, and you can begin to see the lush green field stretching out toward the river.

Arriving at the next corner, you are again stopped by a red light. This time you stand alone and wait. You can feel the pressures of the big city behind you. The towering buildings, the noise, the stale smells, the sense of urgency . . . pressure . . . anxiety and stress.

The light turns green, and you cross the street. Practically jumping over the sidewalk, you land in the soft grass. You can feel the difference in the ground beneath you through your shoes – from the cold hard sidewalk to the warm, plush grass. You've stepped out from the shadows of the buildings and can feel the heat of the sun on your face and arms. Pausing, you raise your arms up in the air, close your eyes and tilt your head toward the sky. The sun splashes over you. You stand there soaking it in.

<PAUSE>

When you open your eyes, it takes a few minutes to be able to fully see what is around you. You begin walking across the green field towards the arching tunnel that is before you. There are groups of people playing frisbee and children chasing bubbles being blown by their parents. Several dogs run after tossed tennis balls. Blankets are sprinkled throughout the field, hosting picnics or people lost in books. You hear laughter and shrieks of joy and barking. After dodging a few flying frisbees and running children, you step into the darkness of the tunnel and walk across the arched footbridge.

Coming out on the other side, you see a huge American flag waving in the breeze to your left. To your right, you see a sidewalk heading to steps that would take you up to the bridge. You look straight ahead. Another bright green field is before you. Clusters of tall trees line either side of the field. There are more groups of friends and family scattered across the grass. You weave your way between them, your eyes on your destination . . . the fountain.

Water soars into the sky. It appears to stop at the highest point before dropping back into the pool below. A slight breeze carries a fine mist to the right. A rainbow appears along the edge of the mist.

You walk down the steps to the base of the fountain. Leaning forward, you place your hands on the cool concrete. Watching the water spray in the air, you can see the individual droplets glistening in the sunlight. Now that you are up close, you see multiple rainbows dancing among the falling water.

Your attention is grabbed by a woman on roller skates gliding past the fountain on the other side. You are now aware of other people moving around you. People on skateboards and riding bikes, and jogging. There are boats floating on the river – some bobbing in the small waves and others zipping along the water. So much movement. So much joy.

You turn your focus back to the fountain. Climbing onto the concrete base, you lay down on your back, placing your feet down next to your bottom so that your knees are bent. At first, you lay there with your eyes closed. You can hear the chatter and laughter of those moving around you. Soon those sounds fade off into the distance, and all you can hear is the roar of the fountain water being thrown up into the sky and then slapping the surface of the pool as it falls back to earth. At times you can feel a fine cool mist brush your face.

<PAUSE>

Slowly you open your eyes. Sparkling beads of water appear to be flying through the bright blue sky. You see fluffy vivid white clouds slowly drifting across the blue canvas above you. Laying here, you feel your body relax. Your mind is completely focused on the beauty before you. You take several deep breaths and lay still, watching this private show of dancing clouds and flying water.

<PAUSE>

It has been a beautiful afternoon. You feel relaxed. You feel rested.

It is time to leave this special place.

Return your focus to your breath.

Take a deep breath in through your nose.

Slowly exhale through your mouth.

Deep breath in.

Exhale.

Deep breath in.

Exhale. Take a deep breath in.

When you are ready, return your focus to the present moment.

Open your eyes.

Wiggle your fingers.

Wiggle your toes.

Face the rest of your day with a heart filled with happiness, joy, and hope.

GUIDED IMAGERY: CLOUDS

I invite you to join me for a Guided Imagery Mindfulness Practice. Allow your body to relax while your mind escapes to the clouds.

Take a deep breath in through your nose.

Slowly exhale through your mouth.

Deep breath in.

Exhale.

Deep breath in.

Exhale.

Allow your body to sink into a comfortable position. If you choose, close your eyes. Rest your hands gently in your lap or at your side. Continue to take deep breaths as you give your entire body permission to relax.

Your forehead.

Your jaw.

Your neck.

Your shoulders.

Your spine.

Your stomach.

Your thighs.

Your ankles.

Relax from your head to your toes.

Focus your attention back to your breathing.

Deep breath in.

Exhale.

Deep breath in.

Exhale.

<PAUSE>

Now picture yourself outside, lying on your back on a soft blanket. You can feel the thick grass under the blanket. The summer sun is shining bright. As you lay there with your eyes closed, the warmth of the sun tickles your face, your arms, and your legs. There is a slight breeze that dances across you.

Suddenly the warmth disappears. Opening your eyes, you see that a large fluffy white cloud has covered the sun. With the sunlight radiating from behind and against the deep blue of the sky, the cloud appears to glow.

Your gaze shifts, and you notice that there are many other clouds in the sky. They are very slowly drifting by you.

Notice the different textures of the clouds as they float lazily through the sky.

There are round cottony clouds.

There are long thin wispy clouds.

Some are vivid white.

Some are almost transparent, like streaks of paint.

Some seem so close you could reach out to touch them.

Others are farther away, appearing to be sinking into the great blue sky.

You feel very relaxed, laying here watching the clouds roll by.

The longer you stare up at the sky, the more the clouds change before your eyes. You can see shapes and objects forming within the clouds. Then they disappear, and the cloud transforms into a new shape.

Let us hold this space for a few moments. It is so peaceful and relaxing to lay here and watch the clouds. What are you seeing? A heart? A rabbit? A boat? Allow those images to float before you slowly.

<PAUSE>

It has been a beautiful afternoon of gazing up at the clouds. You feel rested. You feel relaxed.

Return your focus to your breath.

Take a deep breath in through your nose.

Slowly exhale through your mouth.

Deep breath in.

Exhale.

Deep breath in.

Exhale. Take a deep breath in.

When you are ready, return your focus to the present moment.

Open your eyes.

Wiggle your fingers.

Wiggle your toes.

Face the remainder of your day feeling rested and relaxed.

GUIDED IMAGERY: THE FOREST

I invite you to join me for a Guided Imagery Mindfulness Practice. Allow your body to relax while your mind escapes to the forest.

Take a deep breath in through your nose.

Slowly exhale through your mouth.

Deep breath in.

Exhale.

Deep breath in.

Exhale.

Allow your body to sink into a comfortable position. If you choose, close your eyes. Rest your hands gently in your lap or at your side. Continue to take deep breaths as you give your entire body permission to relax.

Your forehead.

Your jaw.

Your neck.

Your shoulders.

Your spine.

Your stomach.

Your thighs.

Your ankles.

Relax from your head to your toes.

Focus your attention back to your breathing.

Deep breath in.

Exhale.

Deep breath in.

Exhale.

<PAUSE>

Now picture yourself standing at the edge of a forest. You slowly lift your chin, tilting your head back as your eyes scan the trees before you. Deep shades of green melt together as the trees reach far into the air and eventually brush against the bright blue sky. You squint your eyes as the sunlight warms your face. It is a very warm day. You stand here for a minute and take in several deep breaths.

<PAUSE>

Returning your gaze to look straight ahead, you see a path that goes into the woods. All vegetation has been worn away by those who have gone before you. Their adventurous footsteps leave a dirt path that appears to disappear into the trees. You follow their lead and head into the woods.

The farther you walk, the cooler it gets. The canopy of trees keeps the sun from peaking in. You zip up the light jacket you are wearing.

The ground below you is sprinkled with rocks and leaves and small sticks. As you walk, you can hear them crunching beneath you. Every once in a while, your toes connect with a rock sending it rolling ahead of you. Tree roots spring forth from the earth – some small, some sticking higher from the dirt. You need to pay attention to where you step so that you don't trip.

Occasionally, a squirrel or chipmunk darts across the path in front of you. You can hear birds singing as they fly through the trees above.

On either side of you, the ground is covered with moss and ferns, and other plants. Some grow across the forest floor. Others have grown as high as your knees. There are more shades of green than you could even begin to name. It is so beautiful.

The greens are interrupted by the browns of fallen tree trunks and branches. Tree trunks of all thicknesses and textures sprout from the ground. There are many different kinds of trees. All different shapes and sizes.

With each step that you take, you feel any stress or tiredness you are experiencing melting away. You feel your spirit being renewed. Walking through the woods is invigorating.

As you walk, what else do you see?

What do you hear?

What do you smell?

<PAUSE>

The path bends slightly to the left, and you continue to follow it. Ahead you notice a break in the tall trees where sunlight is pouring in, creating a hazy glow within the forest. Off the path, you see that a large tree has fallen. Leaving the path, you walk towards the fallen tree feeling the vegetation brushing against your lower legs. Every once in a while, you need to step over small tree trunks and limbs.

Arriving at the fallen tree, you realize its true enormity. The horizontal trunk is almost as tall as you are! Brushing your hand across the bark, it is cool and rough on your fingertips. Pushing on it, the trunk feels solid. You find a place where smaller trees appear to have been knocked down by this one. The limbs of those trees allow you to climb up on the tree trunk. You find a spot where you can easily lie down. It is wide enough for you to lie there comfortably. You feel the cool hard trunk against your back. You put your hands behind your head and stare up at the bright blue sky visible through the hole in the trees. You can once again feel the warmth of the sun on your face.

You lay here taking in several deep breaths.

What do you see?

<PAUSE>

What do you hear?

<PAUSE>

What do you smell?

<PAUSE>

How do you feel?

<PAUSE>

You stay here for a while, soaking in the peacefulness and relaxation of the forest.

<PAUSE>

It is time to leave this tranquil place.

You slowly lift yourself to sit on the trunk, turning so that your legs are dangling off the side. Carefully, you jump to the ground.

You make your way through the forest's vegetation returning to the path.

Heading back the way you came.

Hearing the leaves and sticks crunch beneath your feet.

Dancing over the rocks and tree roots.

<PAUSE>

Before long, you can see the end of the path before you. Your walk has come to an end.

It is time to return your focus to your breath.

Take a deep breath in through your nose.

Slowly exhale through your mouth.

Deep breath in.

Exhale.

Deep breath in.

Exhale

When you are ready, return your focus to the present moment.

Open your eyes.

Wiggle your fingers.

Wiggle your toes.

Face the rest of your day with a spirit that is renewed and a heart that is filled with peace.

www.ingramcontent.com/pod-product-compliance
Lightning Source LLC
Chambersburg PA
CBHW041928260326
41914CB00009B/1217